keys to healthy Relationships

"Navigating Modern Relationships: Building Resilience in Love and Heartbreak"

Larry B. Rodriguez PhD

Copyright © 2024 Larry B. Rodriguez PhD
All right reserved

Table of content

Introduction:
 - Setting the stage: The landscape of relationships in the digital age
 - Defining heartbreak: Understanding its impact and prevalence

Chapter 1. Understanding Relationship Dynamics:
 - Exploring common issues leading to heartbreak
 - The importance of communication, trust, and mutual respect

Chapter 2. Building a Strong Foundation:
 - Self-awareness and self-care: The keys to healthy relationships
 - Setting realistic expectations and boundaries

Chapter 3. Communication Strategies:
 - Effective communication techniques for expressing needs and resolving conflicts
 - Active listening and empathy: Strengthening connection and understanding

Chapter 4. Navigating Challenges:
 - Addressing common pitfalls and roadblocks in relationships

- Strategies for overcoming jealousy, insecurity, and mistrust

Chapter 5. Healing from Heartbreak:
- Coping mechanisms for dealing with breakup and loss
- Self-reflection and growth: Turning heartbreak into an opportunity for personal development

Chapter 6. Moving Forward:
- Rebuilding trust and confidence in love
- Finding hope and resilience in the face of heartbreak

Conclusion:
- Empowering readers to cultivate healthy, fulfilling relationships in the modern world

Introduction

In today's fast-paced and interconnected world, the landscape of relationships is constantly evolving. From the rise of online dating to the prevalence of social media, modern technology has reshaped how we meet, connect, and interact with one another. However, amidst the convenience and opportunities offered by these advancements, many find themselves navigating a complex maze of emotions, expectations, and challenges in their quest for love and companionship.

Setting the Stage:
In this introduction, we set the stage for exploring the intricacies of modern relationships and the pervasive phenomenon of heartbreak. We acknowledge the prevalence of heartbreak in today's society and its profound impact on your emotional well-being and outlook on love.

Defining Heartbreak:
Heartbreak is more than just the end of a romantic relationship; it encompasses a spectrum of emotions ranging from sadness and grief to anger and confusion. We delve into the multifaceted nature of heartbreak, exploring its causes,

manifestations, and long-term effects on your mental and emotional health.

The Journey Ahead:
As you embark on this journey with us, our goal is to provide insights, strategies, and tools for navigating the complexities of modern relationships with resilience and grace. We invite you to join us in exploring the dynamics of love and heartbreak in the digital age and discovering pathways to healing, growth, and fulfillment.

Empowering You:
Throughout this book, we empower you to cultivate healthy, fulfilling relationships by fostering self-awareness, nurturing effective communication skills, and embracing vulnerability. By offering practical advice, real-life anecdotes, and evidence-based insights, we aim to equip you with the knowledge and confidence to navigate the ups and downs of love with resilience and optimism.

Setting the Stage:

In the digital age, the quest for love unfolds against a backdrop of unprecedented connectivity and constant innovation. Online dating platforms promise an endless array of potential matches, each just a swipe away. Social media platforms offer a window into the lives of others, where carefully curated profiles showcase moments of joy, adventure, and romance. Instant messaging apps facilitate instantaneous communication, allowing us to stay connected with loved ones across time zones and continents.

Yet, beneath the veneer of convenience and accessibility lies a landscape fraught with complexity and uncertainty. The allure of endless choice can paradoxically lead to decision paralysis, as we sift through countless profiles in search of the perfect match. The pressure to present a polished online persona can fuel feelings of inadequacy and self-doubt, as we strive to measure up to the filtered images and curated narratives of others.

Moreover, the digital realm often blurs the boundaries between the public and the private, leaving us vulnerable to scrutiny and judgment from others. What was once reserved for intimate conversations behind closed doors is now laid bare for all to see, inviting commentary and critique from friends, family, and strangers alike. The relentless stream of notifications, likes, and comments can create a constant undercurrent of validation-seeking behavior, as we seek affirmation and approval in the form of digital currency.

In this hyper-connected world, the art of genuine communication and authentic connection can become lost amidst the noise and distractions. Meaningful conversations are replaced by abbreviated texts and emojis, leaving nuances and subtleties lost in translation. Misunderstandings and miscommunications abound, as the immediacy of digital communication leaves little room for reflection and empathy.

Yet, amidst these challenges, there remains a glimmer of hope—a recognition of the profound human longing for connection and intimacy. Despite the pitfalls and perils of the digital age, we continue to yearn for genuine connection, for moments of shared laughter, vulnerability, and understanding. In the midst of the chaos, we cling to the belief that love, in all its messy, imperfect glory, has the power to transcend screens and algorithms, to bridge the divides that separate us and to unite us in our shared humanity.

As we embark on this journey together, let us navigate the complexities of modern relationships with curiosity, compassion, and courage. Let us embrace the opportunities for growth and connection that technology affords, while remaining mindful of the pitfalls and challenges that lie ahead. And above all, let us remember that love, in its purest form, is a testament to the resilience of the human spirit—a force that endures, despite the odds, and reminds us of the beauty and fragility of the human experience.

Defining Heartbreak: Understanding its Impact and Prevalence

Heartbreak is a universal human experience, transcending culture, age, and gender. At its core, heartbreak represents the profound emotional pain and distress that accompanies the loss of a significant relationship. Whether it's the end of a romantic partnership, the dissolution of a friendship, or the rupture of a familial bond, heartbreak leaves an indelible mark on our psyche, reshaping our perceptions of ourselves, others, and the world around us.

The experience of heartbreak is multifaceted, encompassing a wide range of emotions, from sadness and grief to anger and disbelief. It can manifest physically, with symptoms such as insomnia, loss of appetite, and fatigue, as well as emotionally, with feelings of worthlessness, despair, and hopelessness. The intensity and duration of heartbreak vary from person to person, influenced by factors such as the depth of the relationship, the circumstances of the breakup, and individual coping mechanisms.

In today's society, the prevalence of heartbreak is strikingly high, with countless individuals navigating the tumultuous terrain of love and loss. The rise of online dating and social media has opened up new avenues for connection and exploration, but it has also made relationships more transient and disposable. The illusion of endless choice and instant gratification can lead to a lack of commitment and investment in relationships, making heartbreak all the more common.

Moreover, the pervasive influence of media and popular culture perpetuates unrealistic ideals of love and romance, setting unrealistic expectations for relationships and creating a breeding ground for disappointment and disillusionment. From fairy-tale endings to romantic comedies, the narrative of "happily ever after" obscures the messy realities of love, glossing over the complexities and challenges that arise in real-world relationships.

Despite its prevalence and impact, heartbreak is not an insurmountable obstacle. With time, patience, and self-care, individuals can heal from the wounds of heartbreak and emerge stronger, wiser, and more resilient. By acknowledging the pain and allowing ourselves to grieve, we create space for healing and growth, paving the way for new beginnings and opportunities for love and connection.

In the pages that follow, we will explore the myriad facets of heartbreak, from its causes and consequences to strategies for coping and healing. Through personal anecdotes, expert insights, and evidence-based advice, we aim to shed light on this universal human experience and offer guidance for navigating the tumultuous terrain of love and loss.

Chapter 1

Understanding Relationship Dynamics

Relationships are complex and dynamic interactions between individuals, influenced by a myriad of factors such as communication styles, attachment patterns, and shared values. To navigate relationships successfully, it's crucial to understand the underlying dynamics that shape how we relate to one another.

Communication Styles: Effective communication is the cornerstone of healthy relationships. However, individuals often have different communication styles, influenced by upbringing, cultural background, and past experiences. Some may be more expressive and verbal, while others may prefer non-verbal cues or rely on indirect communication. Understanding and respecting each other's communication preferences can foster better understanding and connection in relationships.

Attachment Patterns: Attachment theory posits that our early experiences with caregivers shape our attachment patterns and influence how we relate to romantic partners later in life. Individuals with secure attachment styles tend to feel comfortable with intimacy and autonomy, while those with insecure attachment styles may struggle with trust, dependence, or avoidance in relationships. Recognizing and understanding our own attachment patterns can help us navigate relationship challenges and cultivate secure, fulfilling connections.

Shared Values and Goals: Shared values and goals form the foundation of strong relationships. When partners share similar beliefs, priorities, and life aspirations, they are better aligned to support each other's growth and well-being. However, differences in values or goals can lead to conflicts and misunderstandings if not addressed openly and respectfully. Building a strong foundation of mutual respect and understanding allows partners to navigate differences constructively and work towards common goals.

Power Dynamics: Power dynamics play a significant role in shaping relationship dynamics, influencing decision-making, conflict resolution, and overall satisfaction. Healthy relationships are characterized by equality and mutual respect, with power shared between partners in a balanced and consensual manner. However, imbalances in power can lead to issues such as control, manipulation, or coercion, undermining the integrity of the relationship. Recognizing and addressing power dynamics is essential for fostering trust and fostering a sense of agency and autonomy in relationships.

Emotional Intelligence: Emotional intelligence refers to the ability to recognize, understand, and manage one's own emotions, as well as to empathize with the emotions of others. In relationships, emotional intelligence plays a crucial role in navigating conflicts, expressing needs and boundaries, and fostering intimacy and connection. Partners with high emotional intelligence are better equipped to communicate effectively, resolve conflicts constructively, and build a strong foundation of trust and empathy.

By understanding and navigating these relationship dynamics, individuals can cultivate healthy, fulfilling connections characterized by mutual respect, communication, and empathy. In the following chapters, we will explore practical strategies and tools for enhancing relationship dynamics and fostering thriving partnerships in the modern world.

Exploring Common Issues Leading to Heartbreak

1. Communication Breakdown: Poor communication is a leading cause of relationship problems. When partners struggle to express their needs, listen actively, or resolve conflicts constructively, misunderstandings can escalate, leading to feelings of resentment and disconnection.

2. Lack of Trust: Trust forms the foundation of healthy relationships. When trust is compromised due to lies, betrayal, or secrecy, it erodes the sense of security and intimacy between partners, often leading to heartbreak.

3. Unmet Expectations: Unrealistic or unmet expectations can create tension and disappointment in relationships. Whether it's expecting constant validation, financial support, or emotional fulfillment, when partners fail to meet each other's expectations, it can strain the relationship and ultimately lead to heartbreak.

4. Infidelity: Infidelity, whether emotional or physical, can be devastating to a relationship. The betrayal of trust and breach of commitment can shatter the foundation of the partnership, leaving both partners grappling with feelings of hurt, anger, and betrayal.

5. Mismatched Values or Goals: Partners who have fundamentally different values, priorities, or life goals may find it challenging to sustain a fulfilling relationship. Whether it's differences in religion, career aspirations, or family planning, when partners are not aligned in their vision for the future, it can lead to conflict and ultimately, heartbreak.

6. Lack of Intimacy: Emotional and physical intimacy are essential components of a thriving relationship. When partners become disconnected or neglectful of each other's needs for affection, intimacy, and connection, it can lead to feelings of loneliness and dissatisfaction, ultimately contributing to heartbreak.

7. Addiction or Substance Abuse: Substance abuse or addiction can wreak havoc on relationships, causing emotional, financial, and interpersonal strain. Partners may struggle to cope with the challenges of addiction, leading to feelings of resentment, frustration, and ultimately, heartbreak.

8. Unresolved Conflict: Avoiding or ignoring conflict can lead to resentment and unresolved issues simmering beneath the surface. Over time, these unresolved conflicts can erode the bond between partners, leading to emotional distance and ultimately, heartbreak.

9. Lack of Emotional Support: Relationships thrive on mutual support and encouragement. When partners fail to provide emotional support during times of stress, grief, or adversity, it can create feelings of isolation and loneliness, ultimately contributing to heartbreak.

10. Failure to Grow Together: Individuals and relationships evolve over time. When partners fail to grow together or support each other's personal growth and development, it can create feelings of stagnation and resentment, ultimately leading to heartbreak as partners outgrow each other.

By exploring and addressing these common issues leading to heartbreak, individuals and couples can work towards building healthier, more resilient relationships characterized by communication, trust, and mutual respect.

The Importance of Communication, Trust, and Mutual Respect

1. Communication: Effective communication is the cornerstone of any healthy relationship. It involves expressing thoughts, feelings, and needs openly and honestly, while also listening actively and empathetically to your partner. Good communication fosters understanding, connection, and intimacy between partners, allowing them to navigate conflicts, solve problems, and strengthen their bond.

2. Trust: Trust is the foundation upon which healthy relationships are built. It is the belief that your partner is reliable, dependable, and has your best interests at heart. Trust involves being vulnerable and emotionally open with your partner, knowing that they will respect and support you. Without trust, relationships are fraught with insecurity, jealousy, and doubt, ultimately leading to heartbreak and dissolution.

3. Mutual Respect: Mutual respect is essential for maintaining dignity, autonomy, and equality in relationships. It involves recognizing and honoring each other's boundaries, opinions, and individuality. Partners who respect each other treat one another with kindness, consideration, and empathy, fostering a sense of partnership and solidarity. Without mutual respect, relationships can become toxic and emotionally damaging, eroding the foundation of trust and communication.

In essence, communication, trust, and mutual respect are interconnected pillars that support healthy, fulfilling relationships. When these elements are present, partners feel valued, understood, and supported, fostering a deep sense of connection and intimacy. Conversely, when communication breaks down, trust is compromised, or mutual respect is lacking, relationships suffer, often leading to heartbreak and dissolution.

By prioritizing open and honest communication, nurturing trust, and cultivating mutual respect, individuals can build resilient and thriving relationships characterized by love, understanding, and mutual support.

Chapter 2

Building a Strong Foundation

1. Self-awareness: Before embarking on a relationship journey, it's essential to understand oneself. This involves exploring one's values, beliefs, needs, and boundaries. Self-awareness allows individuals to enter relationships with clarity about who they are and what they seek, reducing the likelihood of mismatched expectations or conflicts down the line.

2. Clarity of Intentions: Being clear about one's intentions and desires for a relationship sets the stage for healthy communication and mutual understanding. Whether seeking a casual connection or a long-term partnership, honest communication about intentions fosters trust and ensures both partners are on the same page.

3. Effective Communication: Communication is the lifeblood of any relationship. Building a strong foundation requires open, honest, and respectful communication. Partners should feel comfortable expressing their thoughts, feelings, and needs, while also actively listening and empathizing with each other. Effective communication promotes understanding, connection, and intimacy.

4. Establishing Boundaries: Boundaries are essential for maintaining autonomy, self-respect, and emotional well-being in relationships. Partners should communicate their boundaries clearly and respect each other's limits. Healthy boundaries create a safe and respectful environment where both partners feel valued and understood.

5. Shared Values and Goals: Aligning values and goals lays the groundwork for a harmonious and fulfilling relationship. Partners should explore and discuss their core values, priorities, and life aspirations to ensure compatibility and mutual understanding. Shared values provide a sense of unity and purpose, fostering a strong sense of partnership and commitment.

6. Respect and Empathy: Mutual respect and empathy are fundamental for building a strong foundation in relationships. Partners should treat each other with kindness, consideration, and understanding, honoring each other's perspectives and feelings. Cultivating respect and empathy creates a supportive and nurturing environment where both partners feel valued and appreciated.

7. Conflict Resolution Skills: Conflicts are inevitable in any relationship, but how they are managed can either strengthen or weaken the foundation. Building strong conflict resolution skills involves listening actively, expressing feelings calmly and respectfully, and seeking mutually satisfactory solutions. Constructive conflict resolution promotes understanding, growth, and deeper connection between partners.

By prioritizing self-awareness, effective communication, mutual respect, and shared values, individuals can lay the groundwork for a strong and resilient relationship. A strong foundation provides a stable framework for navigating the challenges and joys of partnership, fostering a deep and lasting connection between partners.

Self-awareness and Self-care: The Keys to Healthy Relationships

1. Self-awareness: Understanding oneself is a fundamental aspect of nurturing healthy relationships. Self-awareness involves introspection, reflection, and a deep understanding of one's thoughts, feelings, strengths, and limitations. By developing self-awareness, individuals can identify their needs, values, and boundaries, empowering them to communicate effectively and advocate for themselves in relationships. Self-awareness also fosters empathy and understanding towards others, enhancing emotional intelligence and promoting deeper connections.

2. Emotional Regulation: Self-awareness enables individuals to regulate their emotions effectively, a crucial skill in maintaining healthy relationships. By recognizing and managing their emotional responses, individuals can avoid reactive behaviors, such as defensiveness or hostility, and respond to situations with empathy and understanding. Emotional regulation creates a supportive and nurturing environment where partners feel validated and respected, fostering trust and intimacy in the relationship.

3. Boundaries: Self-awareness plays a vital role in setting and maintaining healthy boundaries in relationships. By understanding their own needs and limitations, individuals can communicate their boundaries clearly and assertively, ensuring their emotional and physical well-being is respected. Boundaries create a sense of safety and security in the relationship, promoting mutual respect and trust between partners.

4. Self-care: Prioritizing self-care is essential for nurturing healthy relationships. Self-care involves taking deliberate actions to nourish one's physical, emotional, and mental well-being. This can include practices such as exercise, mindfulness, hobbies, and spending time with supportive friends and family. By prioritizing self-care, individuals replenish their energy and resilience, enabling them to show up fully present and engaged in their relationships.

5. Authenticity: Self-awareness cultivates authenticity in relationships, as individuals feel comfortable being their true selves with their partners. Authenticity fosters trust, intimacy, and connection, as partners can relate to each other from a place of honesty and vulnerability. By embracing authenticity, individuals create an environment where genuine connection and mutual acceptance thrive.

6. Continuous Growth: Self-awareness is an ongoing journey of growth and self-discovery. Individuals who prioritize self-awareness remain open to learning and evolving, both as individuals and as partners in a relationship. This continuous growth fosters resilience, adaptability, and a deeper understanding of oneself and others, enriching the relationship and promoting long-term satisfaction and fulfillment.

By cultivating self-awareness and prioritizing self-care, individuals lay the groundwork for healthy, fulfilling relationships built on mutual respect, understanding, and authenticity. As individuals become more attuned to their own needs and emotions, they are better equipped to navigate the complexities of relationships with grace, empathy, and resilience.

Setting Realistic Expectations and Boundaries

1. Understanding Expectations: Expectations are beliefs or assumptions about how a relationship should unfold or how a partner should behave. While expectations are natural and inevitable in relationships, unrealistic or unspoken expectations can lead to disappointment, frustration, and conflict. It's essential to examine and communicate expectations openly with your partner to ensure they are realistic and aligned with both partners' needs and desires.

2. Communicating Expectations: Effective communication is key to managing expectations in relationships. Partners should feel comfortable expressing their needs, desires, and boundaries openly and honestly. This allows for a mutual understanding of each other's expectations and provides an opportunity to negotiate and compromise when necessary. By communicating expectations proactively, partners can avoid misunderstandings and resentment down the line.

3. Setting Realistic Boundaries: Boundaries are guidelines that define acceptable and unacceptable behavior in a relationship. Setting clear and healthy boundaries is essential for maintaining autonomy, self-respect, and emotional well-being. Boundaries can include physical boundaries (e.g., personal space, physical affection), emotional boundaries (e.g., respecting each other's feelings, avoiding manipulation or coercion), and time boundaries (e.g., setting aside time for individual pursuits and self-care). By setting realistic boundaries, individuals create a framework for respectful and fulfilling relationships.

4. Respecting Each Other's Boundaries: It's crucial to respect and honor each other's boundaries in relationships. This requires active listening, empathy, and a willingness to acknowledge and validate each other's needs and limitations. Respecting boundaries fosters trust, safety, and mutual respect in the relationship, creating a supportive and nurturing environment where both partners feel valued and understood.

5. Navigating Differences: Partners may have different expectations and boundaries based on their unique backgrounds, experiences, and personalities. Navigating these differences requires open-mindedness, empathy, and a willingness to compromise. Partners should engage in respectful dialogue and negotiation to find common ground and establish mutually satisfying expectations and boundaries that honor both individuals' needs and values.

6. Revisiting and Adjusting: Relationships are dynamic and evolve over time, so it's essential to revisit and adjust expectations and boundaries as needed. Life circumstances, personal growth, and external factors may impact the dynamics of the relationship, requiring flexibility and adaptability. Regular communication and reflection allow partners to reassess their expectations and boundaries, ensuring they remain realistic, relevant, and supportive of the relationship's growth and well-being.

By setting realistic expectations and boundaries, individuals create a foundation for healthy, respectful, and fulfilling relationships. Clear communication, mutual respect, and a willingness to negotiate and adapt are essential for navigating the complexities of relationships with grace and integrity.

Chapter 3

Communication Strategies for Healthy Relationships

1. Active Listening: Practice active listening by giving your full attention to your partner when they are speaking. This means making eye contact, nodding to show understanding, and refraining from interrupting. Paraphrase what your partner has said to ensure you understand their perspective before responding.

2. Use "I" Statements: When expressing your thoughts, feelings, and needs, use "I" statements to take ownership of your emotions and experiences. For example, instead of saying, "You always make me feel neglected," try saying, "I feel neglected when we don't spend quality time together."

3. Express Empathy: Show empathy by acknowledging and validating your partner's feelings, even if you don't agree with their perspective. Reflect back their emotions and demonstrate understanding. For example, "It sounds like you're feeling frustrated because you didn't receive the support you needed."

4. Avoid Blame and Criticism: Refrain from blaming or criticizing your partner during communication. Instead of attacking their character or behavior, focus on expressing your feelings and needs constructively. This reduces defensiveness and creates a safer space for open dialogue.

5. Practice Assertiveness: Be assertive in expressing your needs, boundaries, and concerns while also respecting your partner's perspective. Assertiveness involves advocating for yourself in a respectful and non-confrontational manner, ensuring your voice is heard without disregarding the needs of your partner.

6. Seek Understanding: Instead of assuming you know your partner's thoughts or motivations, ask clarifying questions to seek understanding. Validate their experiences and perspectives, even if they differ from your own. This demonstrates respect and fosters deeper connection and empathy.

7. Practice Non-verbal Communication: Pay attention to non-verbal cues such as body language, tone of voice, and facial expressions during communication. Non-verbal communication can convey important messages and emotions that may not be expressed verbally.

8. Set Aside Time for Communication: Dedicate regular time for open and honest communication with your partner. This can be a designated "check-in" time where you discuss important topics or simply a daily ritual of sharing thoughts and feelings.

9. Use Conflict Resolution Skills: Conflict is a natural part of relationships, but it's essential to approach it constructively. Practice active listening, compromise, and problem-solving techniques to resolve conflicts respectfully and collaboratively.

10. Seek Professional Help if Needed: If communication challenges persist or if there are underlying issues impacting the relationship, consider seeking the support of a couples therapist or counselor. A trained professional can provide guidance and tools for improving communication and resolving conflicts effectively.

By implementing these communication strategies, individuals can foster understanding, empathy, and connection in their relationships. Effective communication lays the foundation for healthy and fulfilling partnerships built on mutual respect and trust.

Effective Communication Techniques for Expressing Needs

1. Use "I" Statements: Frame your needs using "I" statements to take ownership of your feelings and experiences. For example, instead of saying, "You never help with household chores," try saying, "I feel overwhelmed when I'm responsible for all the household chores."

2. Be Specific: Clearly articulate your needs and preferences to avoid ambiguity. Provide specific examples and details to help your partner understand what you're asking for. For instance, instead of saying, "I need more support," specify, "I would appreciate it if you could help with meal preparation a few times a week."

3. Be Assertive: Be assertive in expressing your needs, maintaining a balance between being passive and aggressive. Assertiveness involves advocating for yourself respectfully and confidently, ensuring your voice is heard while also respecting your partner's perspective.

4. Focus on Solutions: Instead of dwelling on the problem, focus on finding solutions together. Approach the conversation with a collaborative mindset, seeking common ground and brainstorming ways to address your needs while also considering your partner's needs and concerns.

5. Use Active Listening: Encourage your partner to share their perspective by practicing active listening. Give your full attention, paraphrase what they've said to ensure understanding, and validate their feelings and experiences. This creates a supportive environment for open dialogue and mutual understanding.

Effective Communication Techniques for Resolving Conflicts

1. Stay Calm: Maintain your composure and stay calm during conflict discussions. Take deep breaths, use relaxation techniques if necessary, and refrain from escalating the situation with aggressive or defensive behavior.

2. Take Turns Speaking: Practice respectful turn-taking during conflict discussions to ensure both partners have the opportunity to express their thoughts and feelings. Avoid interrupting or talking over each other, and listen actively to your partner's perspective.

3. Focus on the Issue, Not the Person: Keep the focus on the specific issue at hand rather than attacking your partner's character or personality. Refrain from using blame or criticism and instead focus on expressing your feelings and needs related to the situation.

4. Use "I" Statements: Utilize "I" statements to express your thoughts and feelings about the conflict without placing blame on your partner. This encourages personal responsibility and accountability while fostering empathy and understanding.

5. Seek Compromise: Approach conflict resolution with a willingness to compromise and find mutually satisfactory solutions. Be open to considering your partner's perspective and exploring creative alternatives that meet both of your needs.

6. Take Breaks if Needed: If emotions escalate and productive communication becomes difficult, take a break from the conversation. Agree on a time to reconvene once both partners have had time to calm down and reflect. Use this time to engage in self-care activities or grounding exercises to regain perspective.

7. Seek Understanding: Strive to understand your partner's perspective, even if you disagree with their point of view. Ask clarifying questions, validate their feelings, and express empathy to foster a sense of mutual understanding and respect.

8. Agree to Disagree: Accept that not all conflicts can be resolved to everyone's satisfaction. Sometimes, agreeing to disagree on certain issues is the healthiest option for preserving harmony and respect in the relationship. Focus on finding common ground where possible and respecting each other's differences.

By incorporating these effective communication techniques into your interactions, you can express your needs assertively and navigate conflicts constructively, fostering a deeper understanding and connection with your partner.

Active Listening and Empathy: Strengthening Connection and Understanding

1. Active Listening: Active listening is a communication technique that involves fully engaging with the speaker and demonstrating understanding and empathy. It goes beyond simply hearing the words being spoken to truly comprehending the speaker's message, emotions, and underlying needs. Here's how to practice active listening:

   - Give Your Full Attention: Focus your attention entirely on the speaker, maintaining eye contact and eliminating distractions.

   - Listen Without Interrupting: Refrain from interrupting or interjecting while the speaker is talking. Allow them to express themselves fully before responding.

   - Paraphrase and Reflect: Repeat back what the speaker has said in your own words to confirm understanding and show that you're actively engaged. Reflect their emotions and validate their experiences.

- **Ask Clarifying Questions:** Seek clarification if something is unclear or if you need more information to fully understand the speaker's perspective.

   - **Provide Non-verbal Cues:** Use non-verbal cues such as nodding, smiling, and maintaining an open posture to signal attentiveness and understanding.

2. Empathy: Empathy is the ability to understand and share the feelings of another person. It involves putting yourself in the other person's shoes and viewing the situation from their perspective. Here's how to practice empathy:

   - **Validate Feelings:** Acknowledge and validate the speaker's feelings, even if you don't necessarily agree with their perspective. Show compassion and understanding for their emotional experience.

   - **Express Understanding:** Communicate your understanding of the speaker's emotions and experiences, demonstrating empathy and compassion. Use phrases such as "I understand how you feel" or "That sounds really challenging."

- **Avoid Judgment:** Refrain from passing judgment or making assumptions about the speaker's feelings or experiences. Approach the conversation with an open mind and a non-judgmental attitude.

- **Show Support:** Offer support and encouragement to the speaker, showing that you're there for them and willing to provide assistance or comfort if needed.

- **Share Similar Experiences:** If appropriate, share your own experiences or feelings that relate to what the speaker is going through. This can help foster a sense of connection and mutual understanding.

By practicing active listening and empathy, individuals can strengthen their connection with their partner, deepen their understanding of each other's perspectives, and foster a supportive and nurturing relationship environment. These skills promote trust, respect, and intimacy, laying the foundation for healthy and fulfilling relationships.

Chapter 4

Navigating Challenges in Relationships

1. Open Communication: Maintain open and honest communication with your partner, especially during times of difficulty. Express your concerns, feelings, and needs openly and respectfully, and encourage your partner to do the same. Effective communication allows for a better understanding of each other's perspectives and fosters collaboration in finding solutions to challenges.

2. Practice Empathy: Put yourself in your partner's shoes and try to understand their perspective, feelings, and needs. Show empathy and compassion towards their experiences, even if you don't necessarily agree with them. By demonstrating empathy, you create a supportive and validating environment where both partners feel understood and valued.

3. Focus on Solutions: Instead of dwelling on the problem, focus on finding constructive solutions together. Approach challenges as opportunities for growth and learning, and brainstorm potential solutions collaboratively. Be open-minded and flexible in considering different approaches, and be willing to compromise when necessary to reach mutually satisfactory outcomes.

4. Set Boundaries: Establish clear boundaries to protect your emotional well-being and maintain respect in the relationship. Communicate your boundaries assertively and enforce them consistently, ensuring that both partners understand and respect each other's limits. Boundaries create a sense of safety and security in the relationship, preventing resentment and conflict.

5. Seek Support: Don't hesitate to seek support from trusted friends, family members, or a therapist during challenging times. Having a support network can provide perspective, guidance, and emotional validation, helping you navigate challenges more effectively. Additionally, couples therapy can be beneficial for addressing relationship issues and strengthening communication and connection.

6. Practice Self-care: Prioritize self-care to maintain your physical, emotional, and mental well-being during challenging times. Engage in activities that nourish and replenish you, such as exercise, meditation, hobbies, or spending time with loved ones. Taking care of yourself allows you to approach challenges from a place of strength and resilience.

7. Cultivate Resilience: Cultivate resilience by adopting a positive mindset and viewing challenges as opportunities for growth and learning. Focus on your strengths and previous successes in overcoming obstacles, and remind yourself that you have the capability to navigate challenges together with your partner. Stay hopeful and optimistic about the future of your relationship, even during difficult times.

8. Celebrate Progress: Acknowledge and celebrate the progress you and your partner make in overcoming challenges together. Recognize the efforts you both put into improving communication, resolving conflicts, and strengthening your bond. Celebrating small victories reinforces positive behaviors and fosters a sense of accomplishment and connection in the relationship.

By implementing these strategies, couples can navigate challenges more effectively, strengthen their bond, and emerge stronger and more resilient together.

Addressing Common Pitfalls and Roadblocks in Relationships

1. Communication Breakdown:
   - Lack of effective communication is a pervasive issue in many relationships, often leading to misunderstandings, resentment, and distance between partners. It can manifest in various forms, such as poor listening skills, unexpressed emotions, or avoidance of difficult topics.
   - To address communication breakdown, couples must prioritize open, honest, and empathetic communication. This involves actively listening to each other's perspectives, validating feelings, and expressing thoughts and emotions in a non-confrontational manner.
   - Strategies for improving communication include setting aside dedicated time for meaningful conversations, practicing active listening techniques, and seeking clarification when needed. Couples may also benefit from couples therapy or communication workshops to learn effective communication skills.

2. Unresolved Conflict:

- Conflict is a natural part of any relationship, but when left unresolved, it can fester and escalate, causing deep rifts between partners. Common causes of unresolved conflict include ineffective communication, unresolved resentments, and unwillingness to compromise.

- To address unresolved conflict, couples must approach disagreements with a willingness to understand each other's perspectives and find mutually satisfactory solutions. This may involve practicing empathy, active listening, and assertive communication skills.

- Seeking support from a couples therapist or mediator can provide a neutral space for couples to navigate conflicts constructively and learn healthy conflict resolution strategies. Additionally, couples can establish ground rules for fair fighting, such as avoiding personal attacks and taking breaks when emotions run high.

3. Lack of Trust:

- Trust forms the foundation of a healthy relationship, but it can be easily eroded by dishonesty, betrayal, or breaches of confidentiality. Once trust is damaged, rebuilding it requires time, effort, and consistent behavior.

- To address lack of trust, couples must cultivate transparency, reliability, and accountability in their interactions. This may involve being honest and upfront about past mistakes, demonstrating trustworthy behavior through actions, and communicating openly about concerns and insecurities.
- Building trust requires patience and understanding from both partners, as trust is gradually rebuilt through consistent actions and communication. Couples may benefit from setting mutual expectations and boundaries around trust-building activities, such as regular check-ins and shared experiences that foster connection and intimacy.

4. Mismatched Expectations:
- Mismatched expectations occur when partners have differing beliefs or assumptions about the relationship, leading to disappointment, frustration, and conflict. This can stem from differences in communication styles, upbringing, or cultural backgrounds.
- To address mismatched expectations, couples must engage in open, honest dialogue about their needs, desires, and boundaries. This may involve exploring topics such as commitment, roles and

responsibilities, and future goals to ensure alignment and understanding.

- Compromise and negotiation are essential for navigating differences in expectations. Couples must be willing to find common ground and make concessions where necessary to accommodate each other's needs and values. Regular communication and reassessment of expectations can help prevent misunderstandings and resentment from building over time.

5. Neglecting Self-care:

- Neglecting self-care can have detrimental effects on both individuals and the relationship as a whole. When partners neglect their physical, emotional, and mental well-being, they may become depleted, irritable, or disconnected from each other.

- To address neglect of self-care, couples must prioritize individual and collective well-being through intentional self-care practices. This may involve setting aside time for exercise, relaxation, hobbies, and socializing with friends and family.

- Supporting each other in self-care endeavors can strengthen the bond between partners and foster a sense of mutual respect and understanding. Couples can establish routines and rituals that prioritize self-care, such as weekly date nights, shared meals, or outdoor activities that promote physical and emotional health.

6. Taking Each Other for Granted:
   - Over time, partners may start to take each other for granted, leading to feelings of neglect or unappreciation. This can occur when gestures of love and appreciation become less frequent or are no longer acknowledged.
   - To address taking each other for granted, couples must actively cultivate gratitude and appreciation in their relationship. This may involve expressing gratitude for small acts of kindness, acknowledging each other's efforts and contributions, and regularly expressing love and affection.
   - Couples can establish rituals of connection that reinforce appreciation and acknowledgment, such as daily affirmations, gratitude journals, or shared experiences that celebrate their relationship. By prioritizing gratitude and appreciation, couples can strengthen their bond and create a culture of mutual respect and admiration.

7. Lack of Intimacy:
   - Intimacy encompasses emotional, physical, and sexual closeness in a relationship. When intimacy

wanes, partners may feel disconnected, lonely, or unfulfilled, leading to strain on the relationship.

- To address lack of intimacy, couples must prioritize quality time together and engage in activities that foster emotional and physical closeness. This may involve having meaningful conversations, engaging in affectionate gestures, and exploring shared interests and hobbies.

- Open communication about desires and needs for intimacy is crucial for revitalizing the connection between partners. Couples should create a safe space for discussing intimacy openly and without judgment, allowing for mutual understanding and exploration of ways to reignite the spark.

By addressing these common pitfalls and roadblocks in relationships with intentionality, empathy, and collaboration, couples can strengthen their bond, deepen their connection, and cultivate a healthy, fulfilling partnership.

Strategies for overcoming jealousy, insecurity, and mistrust

Overcoming jealousy, insecurity, and mistrust in a relationship requires understanding the underlying causes and implementing effective strategies to address them. Here are some strategies to help overcome these challenges:

1. Identify Triggers and Underlying Issues:
   - Take time to reflect on the situations, behaviors, or thoughts that trigger feelings of jealousy, insecurity, or mistrust. Understanding the root causes of these emotions can help you address them more effectively.
   - Consider whether past experiences, personal insecurities, or communication issues with your partner contribute to these feelings. Identifying underlying issues is the first step toward overcoming them.

2. Communicate Openly and Honestly:
   - Foster open and honest communication with your partner about your feelings of jealousy, insecurity, or mistrust. Share your concerns and experiences in a non-blaming and non-confrontational manner.

- Be receptive to your partner's perspective and validate their feelings as well. Encourage a supportive and understanding dialogue where both partners feel heard and respected.

3. Build Trust Through Transparency:
- Cultivate trust in your relationship by being transparent and reliable in your actions and communication. Keep your partner informed about your whereabouts, activities, and intentions.
- Avoid secrecy or hiding information, as this can fuel feelings of mistrust. Be open to discussing any concerns or doubts your partner may have, and reassure them of your commitment to the relationship.

4. Challenge Negative Thoughts and Beliefs:
- Challenge negative thoughts and beliefs that contribute to feelings of jealousy, insecurity, or mistrust. Question the validity of these thoughts and consider alternative perspectives.
- Practice positive self-talk and affirmations to build self-confidence and self-esteem. Remind yourself of your worth and the strengths of your relationship.

5. Focus on Building Self-Esteem:

- Invest in activities and practices that promote self-esteem and self-confidence. Engage in hobbies, exercise, or self-care routines that make you feel good about yourself.

- Recognize and celebrate your strengths and accomplishments. Building self-esteem can reduce feelings of insecurity and enhance your ability to trust yourself and your partner.

6. Set Boundaries and Establish Mutual Respect:

- Establish clear boundaries within your relationship to protect your emotional well-being and maintain mutual respect. Communicate your boundaries assertively and enforce them consistently.

- Respect your partner's boundaries as well, and strive to create a relationship dynamic based on trust, understanding, and mutual support.

7. Seek Professional Help if Needed:

- If feelings of jealousy, insecurity, or mistrust persist despite your efforts, consider seeking support from a therapist or counselor. A trained professional can provide guidance, tools, and techniques to address these challenges effectively.

- Couples therapy or relationship counseling may also be beneficial for addressing underlying issues and improving communication and trust in the relationship.

8. Practice Patience and Understanding:
- Overcoming jealousy, insecurity, and mistrust takes time and effort from both partners. Be patient with yourself and your partner as you navigate these challenges together.
- Approach the process with empathy, understanding, and a willingness to support each other's growth and healing. Celebrate progress and small victories along the way.

By implementing these strategies and working together with your partner, you can overcome feelings of jealousy, insecurity, and mistrust, and cultivate a healthier and more fulfilling relationship built on trust, communication, and mutual respect.

Chapter 5

Healing from Heartbreak

Healing from heartbreak can be a challenging and gradual process, but with time, self-care, and support, it's possible to find healing and move forward. Here are some strategies to help you navigate the journey of healing from heartbreak:

1. Allow Yourself to Feel: It's important to acknowledge and validate your emotions during this time. Allow yourself to feel the pain, sadness, anger, or confusion that comes with heartbreak. Suppressing or denying your emotions can prolong the healing process.

2. Practice Self-Compassion: Be kind and gentle with yourself as you navigate through this difficult time. Treat yourself with the same compassion and understanding that you would offer to a friend going through a similar experience. Remind yourself that it's okay to not be okay, and give yourself permission to heal at your own pace.

3. Seek Support: Reach out to trusted friends, family members, or a therapist for emotional support. Talking to someone who understands and empathizes with your experience can provide validation, comfort, and perspective. Don't hesitate to lean on your support network during this time.

4. Engage in Self-Care: Prioritize self-care activities that nourish your physical, emotional, and mental well-being. Take time to rest, eat healthily, exercise, and engage in activities that bring you joy and relaxation. Self-care can help alleviate stress and promote healing.

5. Set Boundaries: Establish boundaries to protect yourself from further emotional harm. This may involve limiting contact with your ex-partner, avoiding triggers that exacerbate your pain, and setting aside time for yourself to focus on healing.

6. Reflect and Learn: Use this experience as an opportunity for self-reflection and personal growth. Reflect on what you've learned from the relationship and the breakup, and identify any patterns or behaviors that you'd like to change or improve in future relationships. Allow yourself to grow stronger and wiser from the experience.

7. Focus on the Present: While it's natural to reminisce about the past or worry about the future, try to focus on the present moment. Practice mindfulness and gratitude to cultivate a sense of peace and acceptance in the here and now.

8. Explore New Interests: Use this time to explore new hobbies, interests, or goals that bring fulfillment and meaning to your life. Engaging in activities outside of your comfort zone can help shift your focus away from the pain of heartbreak and towards personal growth and empowerment.

9. Give Yourself Time: Healing from heartbreak is not a linear process and may take longer than expected. Be patient with yourself and trust that with time, you will gradually heal and find closure. Allow yourself to grieve the loss of the relationship while remaining hopeful for the future.

10. Consider Professional Help: If you're struggling to cope with overwhelming emotions or finding it difficult to move forward, consider seeking support from a therapist or counselor. Therapy can provide valuable tools, strategies, and insights to help you navigate the healing process and emerge stronger from heartbreak.

Remember that healing from heartbreak is a journey, and it's okay to take things one day at a time. Be gentle with yourself, practice self-care, and lean on your support network as you navigate through this challenging time. With patience, self-compassion, and resilience, you will gradually find healing and rediscover joy and fulfillment in your life.

Coping mechanisms for dealing with breakup and loss

Coping with a breakup and loss can be incredibly challenging, but there are coping mechanisms that can help you navigate through this difficult time. Here are some strategies to help you cope with breakup and loss:

1. Allow Yourself to Grieve: Give yourself permission to experience the range of emotions that come with a breakup, including sadness, anger, denial, and even relief. It's normal to feel a mix of emotions, and allowing yourself to grieve the loss of the relationship is an important part of the healing process.

2. Reach Out for Support: Lean on your support network of friends, family members, or a therapist for emotional support. Talking to someone who understands and empathizes with your experience can provide comfort, validation, and perspective during this challenging time.

3. Express Your Feelings: Find healthy outlets for expressing your emotions, such as journaling, art, music, or exercise. Expressing your feelings in a creative or physical way can help you process your emotions and release pent-up energy or tension.

4. Practice Self-Care: Prioritize self-care activities that nurture your physical, emotional, and mental well-being. Make time for activities that bring you joy, relaxation, and fulfillment, such as exercise, meditation, hobbies, or spending time with loved ones.

5. Establish Routine and Structure: Maintain a sense of routine and structure in your daily life to provide stability and a sense of normalcy. Stick to regular sleep, eating, and exercise patterns, and engage in activities that give you a sense of purpose and direction.

6. Limit Contact with Your Ex-Partner: Consider limiting or cutting off contact with your ex-partner, at least temporarily, to give yourself space and time to heal. This may involve unfollowing them on social media, avoiding places where you're likely to run into them, and setting boundaries around communication.

7. Focus on Yourself: Use this time to focus on your own personal growth, goals, and well-being. Invest in self-improvement activities, such as learning new skills, pursuing hobbies, or setting and achieving personal goals that empower and fulfill you.

8. Practice Mindfulness: Practice mindfulness techniques, such as deep breathing, meditation, or yoga, to cultivate awareness and acceptance of your present moment experience. Mindfulness can help you stay grounded and centered amidst difficult emotions and thoughts.

9. Seek Distraction: Engage in activities that provide temporary distraction and relief from your emotions, such as watching movies, reading books, or spending time outdoors. While distraction should not be used as a long-term coping strategy, it can offer temporary relief during particularly difficult moments.

10. Give Yourself Time: Healing from a breakup and loss takes time, so be patient and compassionate with yourself as you navigate through the grieving process. Trust that with time and self-care, you will gradually heal and emerge stronger from this experience.

Remember that coping with breakup and loss is a personal journey, and what works for one person may not work for another. It's okay to experiment with different coping strategies and find what works best for you. Be gentle with yourself, practice self-compassion, and trust that healing is possible with time and support.

Self-reflection and growth: Turning heartbreak into an opportunity for personal development

Turning heartbreak into an opportunity for personal development through self-reflection and growth is a powerful way to find meaning and healing in the midst of pain. Here are some steps to help you transform heartbreak into a catalyst for personal growth:

1. Acknowledge Your Feelings: Begin by acknowledging and accepting your feelings of heartbreak. Allow yourself to feel the full range of emotions, including sadness, anger, confusion, and even relief. Recognize that it's okay to grieve the loss of the relationship and that your feelings are valid.

2. Reflect on the Relationship: Take time to reflect on the relationship and the reasons for its end. Consider what you learned from the experience, both positive and negative. Reflect on the dynamics of the relationship, your own behaviors and patterns, and areas where you may have contributed to its success or downfall.

3. Identify Lessons Learned: Use the breakup as an opportunity for self-discovery and growth by identifying lessons learned from the experience. Consider how the relationship has shaped your values, beliefs, and goals. Reflect on any patterns or behaviors that you'd like to change or improve in future relationships.

4. Practice Self-Compassion: Be kind and compassionate with yourself as you navigate through the healing process. Treat yourself with the same love, understanding, and forgiveness that you would offer to a friend in a similar situation.

Practice self-care activities that nourish your physical, emotional, and mental well-being.

5. Set Personal Goals: Use this time to set personal goals and aspirations for yourself. Consider areas of your life where you'd like to grow or pursue new opportunities. Set specific, achievable goals that align with your values and interests, and create a plan for how you'll work towards them.

6. Explore New Interests: Engage in activities and hobbies that bring you joy and fulfillment. Use this opportunity to explore new interests, passions, or hobbies that you may have put on hold during the relationship. Discovering new aspects of yourself can be empowering and invigorating.

7. Focus on Self-Improvement: Commit to self-improvement by focusing on areas of personal development that are important to you. Whether it's improving your physical health, developing new skills, or enhancing your emotional intelligence, invest in activities that contribute to your growth and well-being.

8. Cultivate Resilience: Cultivate resilience by adopting a positive mindset and viewing challenges as opportunities for growth. Embrace setbacks and obstacles as valuable learning experiences that can strengthen your resilience and perseverance. Trust in your ability to overcome adversity and emerge stronger from the experience.

9. Seek Support: Lean on your support network of friends, family members, or a therapist for emotional support and guidance. Share your thoughts, feelings, and aspirations with trusted individuals who can offer perspective, encouragement, and validation.

10. Embrace the Journey: Embrace the journey of self-discovery and personal growth that comes with turning heartbreak into an opportunity for development. Trust that every experience, both joyful and painful, contributes to your growth and evolution as a person.

By embracing self-reflection and growth, you can turn heartbreak into a transformative experience that leads to greater self-awareness, resilience, and fulfillment in your life. Allow yourself to embrace the journey of healing and personal development, knowing that you have the strength and resilience to navigate through it.

Chapter 6

Moving Forward

Moving forward after a breakup or loss can be a challenging but empowering process. Here are some steps to help you navigate this journey and embrace the future with hope and resilience:

1. Acceptance: Acknowledge and accept the reality of the breakup or loss. Allow yourself to grieve the end of the relationship and the dreams you had for the future. Acceptance is the first step towards healing and moving forward.

2. Letting Go: Release any attachments or lingering feelings that may be holding you back from moving forward. Let go of resentment, anger, or blame towards your ex-partner or yourself. Focus on forgiving and freeing yourself from emotional baggage.

3. Focus on the Present: Shift your focus from dwelling on the past to living in the present moment. Practice mindfulness and gratitude to appreciate the blessings and opportunities that surround you right now. Cultivate a sense of presence and awareness in your daily life.

4. Set New Goals: Use this transitional period as an opportunity to set new goals and aspirations for yourself. Reflect on your values, passions, and dreams, and create a vision for the future that excites and motivates you. Set specific, achievable goals that align with your personal values and interests.

5. Reconnect with Yourself: Take time to reconnect with yourself and rediscover who you are outside of the relationship. Engage in self-care activities that nurture your physical, emotional, and mental well-being. Invest in activities that bring you joy, fulfillment, and a sense of purpose.

6. Expand Your Support Network: Surround yourself with supportive friends, family members, and mentors who uplift and encourage you on your journey. Seek out positive influences and meaningful connections that inspire and motivate you to grow.

7. Embrace Change: Embrace change as a natural part of life and growth. Be open to new experiences, opportunities, and relationships that come your way. Embrace uncertainty with curiosity and optimism, knowing that change can lead to growth and transformation.

8. Learn from the Experience: Reflect on the lessons learned from the relationship and breakup. Consider how the experience has shaped you and what you can take away from it. Use the insights gained to inform your future relationships and personal development journey.

9. Practice Self-Compassion: Be gentle and compassionate with yourself as you navigate through this transition. Treat yourself with kindness, understanding, and forgiveness. Practice self-love and self-acceptance, knowing that you are worthy of happiness and fulfillment.

10. Celebrate Progress: Celebrate your progress and achievements along the way, no matter how small. Acknowledge the steps you've taken towards healing and growth, and celebrate the resilience and strength within you. Each step forward is a victory on your journey of moving forward.

Remember that moving forward is a gradual process that takes time, patience, and self-compassion. Trust in your ability to navigate through this transition and embrace the possibilities that lie ahead. With each step forward, you're creating a brighter and more fulfilling future for yourself.

Rebuilding trust and confidence in love

Rebuilding trust and confidence in love after experiencing a breakup or loss can be a gradual process, but it's possible with time, self-reflection, and intentional effort. Here are some steps to help you rebuild trust and confidence in love:

1. Understand Your Feelings: Take time to understand and process your feelings about love and relationships. Reflect on how the breakup or loss has impacted your trust and confidence in love. Identify any fears, insecurities, or negative beliefs that may be holding you back.

2. Practice Self-Reflection: Engage in self-reflection to explore your past experiences with love and relationships. Consider any patterns or behaviors that may have contributed to past challenges or disappointments. Use this insight to identify areas for growth and improvement.

3. Challenge Negative Beliefs: Challenge any negative beliefs or assumptions you may have about love and relationships. Replace negative thoughts with positive affirmations and beliefs that support your ability to experience love and trust again.

Cultivate a mindset of optimism and openness to new possibilities.

4. Heal from Past Wounds: Take time to heal from past emotional wounds and traumas that may be impacting your ability to trust and love again. Seek support from a therapist or counselor if needed to work through unresolved issues and develop healthy coping strategies.

5. Set Healthy Boundaries: Establish clear boundaries in your relationships to protect your emotional well-being and build trust over time. Communicate your needs, expectations, and boundaries openly and assertively with your partner. Respect your partner's boundaries as well, and strive to create a relationship based on mutual respect and trust.

6. Practice Vulnerability: Allow yourself to be vulnerable and open with your partner about your thoughts, feelings, and insecurities. Share your fears and concerns about trusting again, and allow your partner to do the same. Vulnerability can foster intimacy and deepen your connection with your partner.

7. Focus on Communication: Prioritize open, honest, and transparent communication with your partner. Keep the lines of communication open and address any concerns or doubts as they arise. Practice active listening and empathy to better understand your partner's perspective and strengthen your bond.

8. Build Emotional Intimacy: Invest in building emotional intimacy with your partner by sharing your hopes, dreams, and fears. Create opportunities for meaningful conversations and shared experiences that deepen your connection and foster trust.

9. Celebrate Small Victories: Celebrate the progress you make in rebuilding trust and confidence in love, no matter how small. Acknowledge and celebrate the moments of vulnerability, openness, and connection in your relationship. Each step forward is a testament to your resilience and growth.

10. Stay Open to Love: Remain open to the possibility of love and connection, even as you rebuild trust and confidence in love. Approach new relationships with a sense of optimism and curiosity, knowing that each experience offers an opportunity for growth and connection.

Rebuilding trust and confidence in love is a journey that requires patience, self-awareness, and vulnerability. By taking intentional steps to heal from past wounds, set healthy boundaries, and cultivate open communication and emotional intimacy, you can gradually rebuild trust and confidence in love and create a fulfilling and meaningful relationship.

Finding hope and resilience in the face of heartbreak

Finding hope and resilience in the face of heartbreak can be a transformative journey that leads to growth and healing. Here are some strategies to help you find hope and resilience during this challenging time:

1. Practice Self-Compassion: Be kind and compassionate with yourself as you navigate through the pain of heartbreak. Treat yourself with the same love, understanding, and forgiveness that you would offer to a friend in a similar situation.

Practice self-care activities that nurture your physical, emotional, and mental well-being.

2. Focus on the Present Moment: Stay grounded in the present moment and focus on what you can control right now. Practice mindfulness and gratitude to appreciate the blessings and opportunities that surround you in the present moment. Cultivate a sense of presence and awareness in your daily life.

3. Seek Support: Lean on your support network of friends, family members, or a therapist for emotional support and guidance. Share your thoughts, feelings, and experiences with trusted individuals who can offer perspective, empathy, and validation. Seek out support groups or online communities where you can connect with others who have experienced similar challenges.

4. Find Meaning in the Experience: Look for meaning and purpose in the midst of heartbreak. Reflect on what you've learned from the experience, the strengths you've discovered within yourself, and the opportunities for growth and self-discovery that have emerged. Use the pain of heartbreak as fuel for personal growth and transformation.

5. Cultivate Optimism: Cultivate optimism and hope for the future, even in the face of adversity. Focus on the possibilities and opportunities that lie ahead, rather than dwelling on the past. Trust in your ability to overcome challenges and emerge stronger from the experience.

6. Draw on Past Resilience: Reflect on past experiences of resilience and strength that you've demonstrated in difficult times. Draw on these experiences as a source of inspiration and confidence in your ability to navigate through heartbreak. Remind yourself of the resilience and inner strength that resides within you.

7. Practice Gratitude: Cultivate an attitude of gratitude for the blessings and silver linings in your life, even amidst the pain of heartbreak. Take time each day to express gratitude for the love, support, and opportunities that you have. Gratitude can help shift your perspective and foster a sense of hope and resilience.

8. Set Small Goals: Set small, achievable goals for yourself to focus on as you move forward. Break down larger goals into smaller, manageable steps, and celebrate each accomplishment along the way.

Setting goals can provide direction, purpose, and motivation during challenging times.

9. Embrace Resilience as a Process: Embrace resilience as a journey rather than a destination. Recognize that resilience is not about avoiding or suppressing difficult emotions, but rather about facing them head-on with courage and resilience. Allow yourself to experience the full range of emotions that come with heartbreak, knowing that you have the strength and resilience to navigate through them.

10. Stay Hopeful for the Future: Maintain hope and optimism for the future, even when it feels uncertain or challenging. Trust in the healing power of time, self-reflection, and personal growth. Believe in your ability to create a brighter and more fulfilling future for yourself, filled with love, joy, and resilience.

Finding hope and resilience in the face of heartbreak is a courageous and empowering journey that requires patience, self-awareness, and self-compassion. By practicing self-care, seeking support, finding meaning in the experience, and cultivating optimism and gratitude, you can navigate through heartbreak with resilience and emerge stronger and more resilient than ever before.

Conclusion

In conclusion, navigating through heartbreak can be one of life's most challenging experiences, but it is also an opportunity for growth, resilience, and self-discovery. Throughout this journey, we've explored various strategies for coping with heartbreak, rebuilding trust and confidence in love, and finding hope and resilience in the face of adversity.

We've emphasized the importance of self-care, self-reflection, and self-compassion as essential tools for healing and growth. By practicing mindfulness, gratitude, and optimism, we can cultivate resilience and find meaning in the midst of pain. Seeking support from loved ones, therapists, and support groups can provide comfort, validation, and perspective during difficult times.

As we move forward on our journey of healing and personal development, let us remember that heartbreak is not the end of our story, but rather a chapter in our ongoing journey of self-discovery and transformation. With patience, courage, and perseverance, we can emerge from heartbreak stronger, wiser, and more resilient than ever before.

May we embrace the lessons learned, cherish the moments of growth, and remain hopeful for the possibilities that lie ahead. And may we always remember that love, resilience, and hope have the power to guide us through even the darkest of times.

Thank you for joining us on this journey of healing and growth. May you find peace, joy, and fulfillment in the days to come.

Made in the USA
Las Vegas, NV
11 March 2025